# Hull General Cemetery

## A Short Introduction.

# THE HULL GENERAL CEMETERY

## 1847-1972

### A SHORT INTRODUCTION.

**BILL LONGBONE & PETE LOWDEN**

Copyright © Bill Longbone & Pete Lowden.

# Contents:

1. Introduction — 5
2. Why Was it Needed? — 6
3. Heyday — 8
4. Slow Decline — 11
5. Life After Death? — 12
6. **Some People of Interest Buried in the Cemetery** — 15
    - Henry Hodge — 15
    - Dr. Charles Alfred Lee — 17
    - The Hohenreins — 20
    - John Gravill — 22
    - Zachariah Pearson — 24
    - Thomas Earle — 26
    - Michael Kelly — 27
    - William Day Keyworth — 29
    - Rev. William Clowes — 31
    - William Warden — 33
    - Thomas Thompson — 35
    - John Leak — 37
    - Sir James Reckitt and the Quakers — 38
    - John Fountain and the Workhouse — 40
    - John Westall Widdas — 44
    - John Blundell — 45
    - The Blind Institute — 47
    - Henry Redmore — 49
    - Some Other Notables of Interest — 51
7. Conclusion — 53
8. Bibliography — 54
9. Acknowledgements — 55

# Introduction

The Hull General Cemetery has existed for over 170 years. That perhaps doesn't appear to be a long time. Yet in the history of the town and later city of Hull it is significant. That time scale is longer than most things still here in present day Hull. The Guildhall, The Maritime Museum, Paragon Station and Hull City Hall are youngsters in comparison. The cemetery was here before Hull City AFC, Hull FC or Hull Kingston Rovers were ever thought of. It existed before any of the public parks in Hull were created. It was the first cemetery in Hull and the only privately run one. It was also one of the first garden cemeteries in the country.

It cannot be stressed strongly enough how important it is historically and not only just to the City of Hull. It is also nationally important, with it containing the last resting places of such people as Sir James Reckitt of Reckitt and Colman fame and Reverend William Clowes, the originator of Primitive Methodism as well as many others.

It is also a civic resource, important as a charming piece of 'woodland' within the city. This booklet will give the reader some basic information regarding this site and some of its more famous occupants. It is hoped the booklet may generate the desire in the reader to learn more and perhaps encourage them to want to help protect and preserve this vital resource for future generations.

A bibliography is included to assist further research.

# Hull General Cemetery

## Why Was It Needed?

Since before the Middle Ages every person, except for suicides, criminals and other odd exceptions, had the right to be buried in their parish church or, more likely, its graveyard, under common law. Burial grounds, being of limited space, began to fill up, often to the point that the churches looked as if they had been built in a valley. Up to the late 18$^{th}$ century the method of providing more burial spaces was to wait for the body to decay and then, when disarticulation had taken place, the body would be exhumed and the bones would be placed in either the crypt of the church or its charnel house.

This system worked reasonably well nationally until the population boom of the late 18$^{th}$ century began to place stress on it. Locally, Hull and neighbouring Sculcoates were estimated in 1767 to have a joint population of 12,964; by 1792 this had risen to 22,286. In effect the population almost doubled in 25 years. By 1851 the population stood at 95,000. In Hull both parish churches had opened up new burial grounds late in the 18$^{th}$ century in an attempt to manage the increased number of deaths that the burgeoning population created but within a few decades the seams were bursting once again.

Around this time, especially in towns and cities, there were horror stories reported in the press as to the state of the parish burial grounds. Hull was no different to other urban areas. In the 1840s various incidents regarding the crowded and foul state of the burial grounds in Hull, along with anecdotal evidence of gravediggers

*Fig 1. Print of the Cemetery by Bevan in 1848.*

pulling skulls out of graves by their hair, of young boys playing with human skulls and of course the perennial presence of rats and dogs in such areas made people yearn for a better way to treat their loved ones in death.

Co-incidentally, there had developed a movement centred in Western Europe that hoped to deal with this problem. The idea of the garden cemetery was born. In such a cemetery the dead would be buried with grace and dignity, the burial place would be preferably placed outside of the urban area, it would be tastefully laid out with its grounds well planted and stocked whilst also being maintained to a high standard. It would become a place where the living could not only visit the last resting place of their relatives but also enjoy the experience, which was something they could not do in the crowded parish burial grounds.

Norwich was the first urban area to plan such a cemetery with Liverpool quickly following suit but Manchester was the first to actually open such a planned cemetery at Rusholme Road in 1821. The Norwich and Manchester cemeteries were prompted by the need for Dissenters, that is people who did not accept the Anglican Church, to be buried within an un-consecrated burial ground and this factor was also important in Hull, a noted Dissenter town. By 1845 it had become evident that Hull needed a cemetery to cater for both the needs of the Dissenters and also to provide a more dignified burial for all of the dead of the town. Accordingly, a prospectus for one was widely advertised in the local press asking for people to buy shares in this venture. After one or two difficulties the Hull General Cemetery Company was born and began to undertake burials in the April of 1847. The mayor officially opened it in the June of that year.

When it opened it was situated outside the town, in what was then part of the parish of Cottingham. It initially was comprised of 19 acres although at first the company only laid out and planted the first ten acres. The entrance was placed at the junction of Spring Bank with Newland Tofts Lane (now Princes Avenue). The initial plans for the cemetery set out an entrance lodge, a chapel and 'dead house' the latter fulfilling the role of mortuary. Later in its life two further chapels, one Anglican and one Non-Conformist, were built and also two cottages, either side of the lodge, were added. The Hull General Cemetery Company was intent on sending out a statement that here was a new way of dealing with the town's dead and that Hull was abreast if not ahead of the latest fashions. The future looked promising.

*Fig.2. Pre-1877 photograph of the Lodge and Cemetery Gates.*

## **Heyday.**

One of the things that made the Hull General Cemetery stand out amongst burial places in Hull when it opened was that it accepted burials from any faith. Indeed, as mentioned earlier, this was a central aspect of the notion of 'general' cemeteries; that they were non-denominational and were not tied to a parish or parishes. Only certain parts of the original site were consecrated so that other areas in the cemetery could accommodate the non-conformists of which Hull had a good proportion. Amongst such groupings were The Society of Friends also known as Quakers, Methodists, Presbyterians and even at one stage there were proposals for a Jewish section. It also made arrangements with the local Poor Law Commissioners representing the Hull Workhouse, that was situated on Anlaby Road, to bury the paupers that died 'on the parish'. Whether this was good business sense was open to question, although it did constitute a regular income. What it did do, however, was to make Hull General Cemetery Company all-embracing and as such it raised its profile above the other alternatives on offer in Hull at that time.

The grounds of the cemetery were tastefully planned and planted out by the first superintendent, Mr John Shields, in conjunction with Cuthbert Broderick. John Shields, had fulfilled the same role at York General Cemetery when it opened in the 1830s and was obviously not only experienced but eminently qualified for this post. It was noted in the local press of the day that the cemetery grounds were on a par with the Botanical Gardens situated elsewhere in Hull.

Obviously, being a private cemetery company, with shareholders, the company was always seeking a profit and undertook to provide the entire care that one could wish for in the event of a loved one's death. If you wished, and could afford it, the company sold you the grave plot, provided the funeral carriage and entourage, the minister to officiate, the gravedigger to dig and bury the loved one and finally they could also provide you with the headstone or monument of your choice to be placed on the grave. Naturally, as aftercare for the bereaved, they could plant the grave with flowers or shrubs, and also maintain the grave and monument too. If you could afford it of course.

The cost of burial varied with how much you cared to pay. It ranged from a pauper burial at 10 shillings (50p), up to the catacomb burial costing £105, which would probably be the equivalent in 2018 terms of about £7,000 to £9,000. The average income for a labourer in Victorian times was about £1 to £1.50 a week.

The first test of the worth of the new cemetery took place within two years of its opening. Cholera was an endemic disease in its home area of the Bay of Bengal. However, it had begun to be transported around the world unwittingly by English traders and soldiers who had been in that area. The first cholera pandemic swept across Europe in 1830/1, reaching Hull in 1832 from Sunderland. It found the filthy living conditions that the working class in Britain had to endure a perfect spot to multiply and it infected thousands nationwide. Eventually the disease died out and apart from a few houses in the densest areas of population in Hull being whitewashed, little changed.

The second and more deadly cholera pandemic came in 1849 with it reaching Hull in the July travelling overland from Goole via Hamburg. The authorities had taken little heed of the last epidemic and the conditions that some people were living in were dreadful. In some of the courts and alleys of the old town, 20 or 30 families had access to running water via one standpipe, whilst their sanitary needs were met by two or three 'privies' at the end of the block. The 'privies' themselves were not connected to any sewers and workmen emptied them irregularly. These conditions were not unusual. There is little wonder that cholera spread so quickly in the town. By September the death toll was running into thousands.

One of the bright spots of this dark time was that Hull could call upon the Hull General Cemetery for the safe disposal of the dead. If the town had still depended upon the parish burial grounds, the death toll would almost certainly have been higher. The resident non-conformist minister to the cemetery, the Reverend James Sibree, wrote a telling account of this time and how the dead were buried in the cemetery. He stated that the sheer number of funeral hearses often stretched from the Beverley Road and Spring Bank corner up to the very gates of the cemetery. In his memoirs he told of one day when he officiated at 43 burials. This may give some idea of the death toll taking place within the town at this time. At the end of the epidemic some 3% of the population of Hull had died from it, which proportionally was the highest of any town or city in the country.

It was mooted, when the disease had finally burnt itself out, that a monument should be erected on the spot where so many of the victims were buried. This monument, a large obelisk upon a square plinth, was commissioned by the cemetery company and may still be seen today. Hull City Council refurbished it in 2002.

*Fig 3. The Cholera Monument, 2016.*

By the 1850's the cemetery was well established and it became, not only a peaceful and hygienic place for the dead to be buried in, but also a pleasant place to stroll for the town's inhabitants. Indeed, before the opening of the People's Park, now Pearson's Park, in 1861 it was the only place where people could promenade without paying a fee. As such it was immensely popular as a backdrop to the middle classes socializing. We may find this rather strange today but the Victorians appeared to rather enjoy the idea of melancholy for its own sake and a number of people of the period wrote correspondence to the local newspapers stating how much they enjoyed a walk in the cemetery. Indeed, the pressure was so intense that the cemetery company had to change its rules and open the cemetery on a Sunday simply to meet demand from the public.

Of course, at this time, it was also the place to be seen whilst dead too. The more prosperous and important citizens of the town began to opt for burial there. Larger and more ostentatious monuments were erected which we can still see today.

In 1855 intra-mural burials, that is burials taking place within a parish or church burial ground, were prohibited by legislation and Hull General Cemetery now held, with just a few minor exceptions, the monopoly of burials within Hull. For the next few years the Hull General Cemetery was, as they say, the only game in town.

## **Slow Decline**

Unfortunately, the very legislation that removed the previous competitors to Hull General Cemetery also paved the way for its downfall. One of the major aims of this legislation was to allow local authorities to set up their own Boards of Health. Most local authorities moved to do this. Initially seen as a means to avoid the spread of diseases such as cholera and typhoid within the tenements of Victorian cities and towns, to begin with the local authorities concentrated upon improving sanitation and housing.

However, the Act also allowed local authorities to create their own Burial Boards. In Hull this body initially negotiated with the cemetery company to purchase grave spaces within the cemetery grounds but it quickly moved to lease and then purchase from the company the western part of the Hull General Cemetery's land. This purchase occurred in 1862, and although this piece of land was still administered by the Hull General Cemetery Company, this was the beginning of the present Western Cemetery. This was the first of Hull's municipal burial grounds and, by its very nature, did not have to make a profit as it was funded by the public purse. A point not lost on the cemetery company.

Throughout the 1870's and 1880's the annual shareholders' meetings are peppered with statements implying that the local authority was undercharging for its graves and therefore making the cemetery company's charges uneconomic, implying that the rate payer was being 'swindled.'

What these meetings also show however is that the company continued to pay out large dividends to its shareholders whilst not investing in any new land for burial. In 1854 a proposed extension to the north was mooted to cover roughly the area that Welbeck Street now stands upon. Indeed, the cemetery company went so far as to secure a private Act of Parliament to achieve this end. However, these plans came to nothing and, as mentioned above, the company had leased out and then sold its westernmost holdings. In effect it could only expand to the north and it failed to grasp that opportunity.

Looking back, it almost seems, even at this early stage of its life, as if the Cemetery Company realized that the game was up and aimed to gather as much money from the venture whilst the going was good. That profit in a venture like this depended upon selling new graves must quickly have been evident and without the land available for new burials that simply could not happen. The company's failure to expand is hard to understand in those terms and one must draw the conclusion that the directors had seen the writing on the wall for their enterprise. As such, in hindsight, the seeds of the cemetery's decline were sown within a decade of its opening.

The busiest burial period for the cemetery was in the decade 1870 to 1880. In 1887 there were almost 9,000 burials, a peak that was never reached again. In 1897 there were just over 5,000 burials and the $20^{th}$ century saw the numbers dwindle still further until the cemetery eventually closed with the final burial taking place in 1972.

One could argue that the decline had set in earlier with the failure of the Company to invest in further expansion but now the decline began to be felt, and more importantly, seen in other ways. The decision to sell the Princes Avenue frontage to builders in the first decade of the $20^{th}$ century was simply the first indication of retrenchment. The decision to demolish the lodge designed by Cuthbert Broderick, to close the original entrance and create another one less grand further along Spring Bank West in the 1920's highlighted that the cemetery company was retreating and the following 50 years from then appears to be a process of scarcely managed decline until its demise in the early 1970's.

**Life after Death?**

*Fig.4. Photograph displayed in The Hull Daily Mail, 1973.*

The Hull General Cemetery Company sought liquidation via the courts which it achieved in 1972 leaving the site without ownership. Eventually, after questions asked in Parliament the site was sold to Hull City Council for a nominal sum of £1 in 1974. At the time the local press was calling the site an 'eyesore' and demanding that it was cleaned up. What the aims of the council were when it acquired the land initially is open to question and it could be argued the local authority was reacting to events rather than having a strategic goal for the site.

However, within a short space of time the local authority made clear that the cemetery should be re-developed. There had been earlier demonstrations of cemetery 're-development' in the city when Trippet Street, Division Road and the Drypool graveyards in the early 1960s and 70's suffered this process. Redevelopment in this sense meant that the vast majority of headstones would be removed and the cemetery landscaped. This took the form of harrowing and grass seeding the ground so that it could be mown.

Public opposition to this plan for Hull General Cemetery, including such names as Philip Larkin and John Betjeman, was overruled and the wholesale destruction of irreparable historical artefacts took place. The whole process took about 18 months. However, because of Hull General Cemetery's conspicuous role in Victorian Hull, a number of headstones, principally of more notable members of the public, were allowed to remain. Also, as an indication of how 'bad' the cemetery had become until the council stepped in, a number of rows of headstones were left in situ. These are the rows next to and surrounding the Quaker plot. By 1979 the site had been 'developed'.

At first the council maintained the grounds. Grass cutting took place on a regular basis and paths were re-laid every year with sand and gravel. The council maintained the trees. The cemetery resembled a park with headstones dotted around. Children played there, families picnicked and dogs were walked. Apart from the headstones, the cemetery may well have been, to a casual observer, either West Park or Pearson's Park.

Unfortunately, over time, with the council suffering significant funding cuts, the maintenance of the cemetery fell by the wayside and it began to acquire a neglected feel. The dumping of rubbish began to happen more regularly, paths became quagmires; sycamore saplings began to destroy the remaining stones whilst ivy swamped them. The entire cemetery was quickly becoming a place to avoid rather than to visit.

However, a group of like-minded people from all walks of life have recently set up a group called the Friends of Hull General Cemetery, with the aim of rescuing this vital part of our city's heritage. During its short life it has generated a significant amount of interest in the cemetery from the general public and plans are afoot to bid for local and national funding to make the cemetery a more hospitable place for the community to visit yet still retain its historical significance and environmental importance for future generations.

*Fig.5. George Milner's monument, one of the original directors of the cemetery company.*

# Some People of Interest Buried in the Cemetery

## Henry Hodge (1812 – 1889)

*Fig.6. A bust of Henry Hodge in The Guildhall, Hull.*

Born at Kilnsea in 1812, the son of a small farmer and one of 12 children, Henry Hodge was truly a self-made man. In 1826 the Hodge family moved to Hull and took on a dairy farm at Newland Tofts. As a young man Henry worked at Bell's Flour Mill on Holderness Road, which was situated near what is now Morrill Street, the access to the mill being down a track that eventually became the entrance to the clinic.

With seed crushing becoming more and more important in Hull, the mill changed from a flour mill to a seed-crushing mill. Around 1831 the hydraulic press was invented for crushing seed, and soon replaced the old stamper mill (the firm of

Rose, Down & Thompson was one of the early fore-runners in this development). Having accumulated a little capital whilst working at a mill in Louth, Henry along with his brother William, who was now a foreman at Bell's Mill, purchased a former mustard and flour mill, on what was William Street (later Hodge Street) in Drypool, and installed two hydraulic presses.

In 1852 the nearby Tower Mill at the junction of Holderness Road and Clarence Street was purchased, but although the business was successful, the two brothers dissolved the partnership. Henry married Jane Simpson in 1842 and had six children, one of whom was Emma Hodge, who married Joseph Robson. Emma was a very active member of the Primitive Methodist church.

The family originally lived in East Parade on Holderness Road between Williamson Street and Field Street. They also lived and worked at Blaydes House at 6 High Street. In 1869 his daughter Emma died at the young age of 32, which devastated Henry. His wife, Jane, died in 1867 aged 54 years, and in 1871 Henry married his housekeeper, Emma Graves.

Henry's business continued to expand, and he erected the huge Alexandria Mill in High Street. In 1884 he purchased the adjoining Phoenix Mill, followed three years later by the Globe Mill on Church Street, which was part of what is now Wincolmlee.

Henry was also a pioneer in the seed crushing industry, as prior to 1861, the only seeds imported into Hull for oil and cake were linseed, rapeseed and Niger seed, but Henry began to experiment with Egyptian cottonseed, and found that it made an ideal oil for use in the manufacture of soap, paint, culinary purposes and also for cattle feed, and it soon became one of the major seed imports into the town. He subsequently purchased Bell's Mill near Morrill Street, where he had previously worked. The family lived at Ivy House next to the mill.

Like all members of his family, he was also a very active member of the Primitive Methodist Church in Hull, a benefactor of many good causes, and subscribed to the erection of several churches, including the Holderness Road chapel near Bright Street, and the Henry Hodge Memorial Chapel in Williamson Street. He was also a member of the East Hull Conservative Club and an alderman. His brother William was twice mayor of Hull. Henry, his wives Jane & Emma, daughter Emma, son Edwin and son-in-law Joseph Robson are all buried in the 'Prim Corner' (see p.43) of Hull General Cemetery. His brother, William Hodge, and his family also have a large monument in the cemetery.

*Fig.7.Henry Hodge's monument.*

# Dr Charles Alfred Lee (1825-1912)

Born in Hull in 1825 to Hill Lee, a Hull merchant's clerk and his wife Jane Richardson, Dr Charles Alfred Lee originally had a practice at the corner of Worship Street and Mason Street, where the Hull History Centre is currently located. Charles worked on one of the hospital ships moored in the Humber during the cholera epidemic of 1848-9. He moved to No.1 Pryme Street in the 1860s, where he resided and ran his surgery, and was known as the 'oldest medical practitioner in Hull'. He had a philanthropic interest in charitable institutions, including the Toft's Charity, Trinity House Alms-houses on Anlaby Road, Eleanor Scott's Charity and the Sailors' Orphan Homes, as well as being on the board of Hull Royal Infirmary, for which he had helped develop into one of the country's leading teaching hospitals.

He sponsored one of the houses on the Newland Orphan Homes site, which is still known as Dr Lee's House. It was perhaps his first-hand experience of seeing hard-working people becoming impoverished, through no fault of their own when becoming ill, that inspired his benevolence.

Dr Lee never married or had children, and his siblings predeceased him by many years; he therefore had no immediate family. When he died of throat cancer in 1912 aged 86, he left the majority of his considerable wealth of almost £200,000 (£20m at today's value) and 4 ½ acres of land at the corner of Anlaby High Road and Pickering Road for the building of alms-houses for the elderly. They were to be called Lee's Rest Houses in Dr Lee's honour.

Fig.8. Dr. Lee

Hull architect Henry Hare drew up the plans for a series of 16 detached blocks, each containing eight flats arranged around a garden quadrangle, and they were erected during 1914/15. The criteria for entering the Rest Houses was that the residents should be from the Hull area and 'have once been in better circumstances, but through misfortune or sickness have been reduced to poverty or comparative poverty'. The Rest Houses still exist as a charity today.

Dr Lee is buried in Hull General Cemetery in a family grave along with his mother Jane, her sister Elizabeth Richardson and his two brothers, Matthew and Edward. The headstone no longer exists, as it was removed in the 1970's clear-up.

A superb portrait of Dr Lee, painted by the renowned local artist Fred Elwell, still hangs in the Rest Houses on Anlaby High Road, along with the memorial to him in the grounds. Dr Lee was described, in his obituary in the Hull Daily Mail in 1912, as a man of 'quiet benevolence, who disliked publicity'. This seems to aptly describe a man who had been a doctor in Hull for over 50 years and who was still attending to his patients up to the ripe old age of 85.

*Fig.9. Photograph of Lee's Rest Homes, 2017.*

# The Hohenreins

*Fig.10. The Hohenrein monument.*

Above is the vault of the Hohenreins and, as the name suggests, it holds the bodies of a family of German extraction. George Frederick, the founder of the dynasty, came to Hull in the 1840's, aged about 16. He worked as a pork butcher, firstly for others and then finally setting up in business for himself. He was very successful, establishing a string of shops, one of which was at 22, Princes Avenue, a very salubrious part of the town at that time.

He lived at Derringham Cottage, a large house situated on the corner of Victoria and Derringham Street. When he died he left between £60,000 and £70,000, which would have been quite a few millions today.

His second son, Charles Henry, inherited the business after the eldest son moved back to Germany. The family and the business suffered after the outbreak of war in 1914 and Charles and other Germans living in Britain were viewed with suspicion. Threatening letters were sent to the family, especially after the Zeppelin raids on Hull, and shops were attacked. Even though Charles was a serving officer in the East Riding Yeomanry, he was still targeted.

Eventually he had to change the family name to Ross and had a card specially printed and signed by the chief constable to prove he was British. A similar card was placed in his shop windows. One must remember that the Royal Family too had to change their name in this period, due to the heights the xenophobia reached.

Later in life Charles became a director of Hull City AFC and a part owner of many of the cinemas in Hull and Beverley. He died in 1974 and was cremated. His ashes were probably the last interment to take place in the cemetery.

*Fig.11. Close up of the monument showing Charles Henry Ross's interment date.*

# John Gravill (1802-1866)

The stone below actually tells its own story and was erected by public subscription. Apprenticed as a boy on a whaler, John Gravill worked his way upwards in that dangerous career until finally reaching the post of captain by 1849. As can be imagined, working in a demanding and sometimes extremely dangerous business, John had some narrow escapes. The biggest risk appeared to have been the possibility of the ship becoming trapped in the ice and this happened to John on a number of occasions. By 1866 the once large whaling industry in Hull had been reduced to two ships; the Truelove and the Diana, John captained the latter.

In February of that year he sailed the Diana for the whale-hunting grounds but the ship became trapped in the ice. The crew had to be placed on short rations and then even shorter ones. For six months the ship was icebound and in all, finally returned home to Hull after 14 months at sea. Many of the crew suffered terribly with frostbite and eight died from scurvy.

However, the major loss was the captain himself. John Gravill died on the 26$^{th}$ of December 1866 in his cabin. His body was sewn up into canvas and was finally brought back to Hull for burial. At his funeral some of the pallbearers were said to be harpooners who had sailed with him. The funeral itself was said to have attracted over 15,000 attendees according to the local press of the time. The stone was designed and erected by the local stonemason and sculptor W.D. Keyworth. The Diana itself came to a tragic end some three years later off the Lincolnshire coast and with its loss, the whaling industry of Hull finally ended.

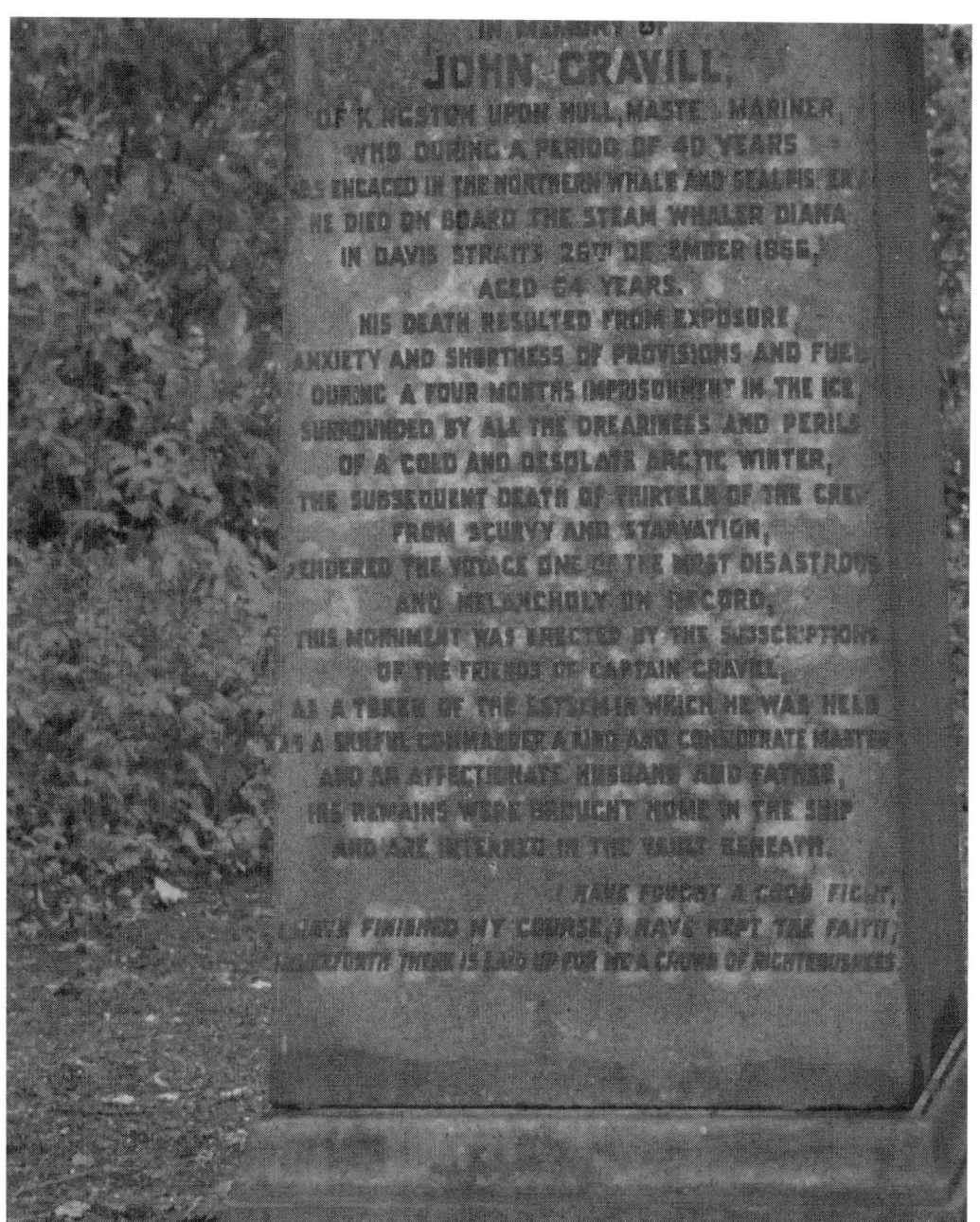

*Fig.12. John Gravill monument, 2017.*

CAPT. GRAVILL.

Fig.13. Image of John Gravill.

## Zachariah Pearson (1821-1891)

Another of the many notables buried in the cemetery, he is justly famous for donating the land to the town that eventually became the first public park in Hull which was later named after him. However, his stone is quite simple and small in comparison to many others and this may be contrasted with the ironstone pillar in Pearson Park with a bas-relief of him attached to it. This contrast is probably due to his fall into disgrace after he went bankrupt in the 1860's. The Victorians could forgive many sins but poverty was not one of them.

Zachariah was always of an adventurous nature. When he was 12, he stowed away on a merchant ship but was caught and returned home. On leaving school, he became an apprentice on a merchant ship and was second officer by the age of 17. He was a captain by the age of 21 and by the age of 25, he owned his own vessel. He spotted a lucrative niche in transporting passengers as well as goods and his business flourished. His rise in the Borough of Hull was just as rapid. Elected a councillor in 1856 and sheriff in 1858, he eventually became mayor in 1859.

Whilst mayor he initiated the planning and building of the new town hall. In 1859 he bought 37 acres on what was then the edge of the town and gave 27 of them to the borough as a park. This was opened with great fanfare in August 1860.

It was shortly after this that he made the strategic mistake of trying to import cotton from the Southern States during the American Civil War, when their ports were being blockaded by the Northern States' fleets. His idea could possibly be justified on one level as the raw cotton from America was the lifeblood of the cotton industry in Britain and due to this blockade, many people, in Hull and especially in Lancashire, were suffering as a result.

*Fig.14. The simple headstone of Zachariah Pearson, 2016.*

Unfortunately, what Zachariah wanted to trade for the cotton were armaments, which the North would never have countenanced. This venture of Zachariah's lost him his entire fleet of ships within the space of two years and he was declared a bankrupt by 1864. This bankruptcy meant that he resigned as mayor during his second term of office. Six months after being declared bankrupt he had cleared all of his debts but he would never seek municipal honours again and contented himself with providing for his family. When Prince's Avenue was opened in 1875 he was invited, as an honorary guest, to the ceremony, an indication that, finally, Victorian Hull had forgiven him.

*Fig.15. Ironstone pillar in Pearson Park, 2016.*

# Thomas Earle (1810-1876)

Born in 1810, the son of John, he began his career as his father's apprentice at the age of 12. He quickly gained a reputation as a master craftsman and one of his first works commissioned was that of Dr Alderson, whose statue still stands outside the Hull Royal Infirmary. Of course, someone of his talent would not be satisfied with the commissioned work that Hull could provide and so he went to London and established himself, gaining work from patrons and some commissions from the Royal Academy. In 1839, still in his twenties, he was awarded the Gold Medal by the Royal Academy.

*Fig. 16. Tomb of Thomas Earle, 2016.*

By the time of the Great Exhibition in 1851 he was so well established that he had three entries placed there. In 1863 he was given the commission to carve the statute of Queen Victoria that stands in Pearson Park. The complementary statue of her husband, Prince Albert sited across the park, was also carved by this gifted artist. There are many other examples of his work still extant within the city.

*Fig.17. Thomas Earle as a young man.*

# Michael Kelly (1864-1949)

Michael Kelly was born at the Curragh army barracks in Ireland on 24 May 1864, the eldest son of Sgt Michael Kelly and Elizabeth Partridge. After serving in India and South Africa, Sgt Kelly and his family moved first to Beverley Barracks and then to Hull in 1869 where they lived in the Anlaby Road/Spring Bank area of Hull. Michael trained as a clerk with Mr Edward Nequest of the Hull General Cemetery, and married Susanna Barner in 1890. They had three children, Ann (1890), Michael John (1892) and Louis (1894).

On the retirement of Edward Nequest, Michael became the secretary and superintendent of the Hull General Cemetery in November 1892. The family lived at the lodge in the cemetery. He developed a system for recording the burials and their location methodically keeping accurate records of each burial and details of the deceased. This information has proved invaluable to modern researchers, enabling specific graves to be identified.

His wife Susanna died in 1896 aged just 29, leaving him to look after the young children. The following year he married a widow, Emily Walker Lancaster (nee Vacare), and had a daughter, Cecilia Mary (Cissie) in 1899. Sadly, tragedy was to befall him again, when his son Louis died of appendicitis in 1903 aged nine. His elder daughter, Ann, didn't marry, but his younger daughter, Cissie married, and had a daughter, Monica Joan.

At the outbreak of WW1 his son, Michael John, joined the East Yorkshire Regiment as a Lewis Gunner and was promoted to Lance Corporal. Sadly, he was killed at the Battle of Kemmell on Easter Day, 22 April 1916, aged 23. He is buried at Lindenhoek Chalet Military Cemetery in Belgium and commemorated on the family grave in Hull General Cemetery.

*Fig.18. Michael Kelly with his wife and daughter standing to the rear of the cemetery lodge.*

Michael continued to work at the cemetery and was involved with it until his death in 1949 aged 84. He is buried in Hull General Cemetery along with his father, mother, first wife, his mother-in-law and his son Louis. The memorial still remains.

We all owe him a great debt for the work he did in producing detailed plans and accurately recording the burials in Hull General Cemetery.

## William Day Keyworth (1843-1902)

In addition to the many busts and sculptures located in The Ferens Art Gallery and The Hull Guildhall, the prominent Hull sculptor, William Day Keyworth, was responsible for many of the public statuary in Hull, such as William de la Pole in Nelson Street, Andrew Marvell in Trinity Square and William Wilberforce in the gardens of Wilberforce House.

He was born in Hull, the son of William Day Keyworth Snr (1818-1897), also an eminent sculptor, undertaking many public works, especially in Leeds. William Day Keyworth lived with his wife Elizabeth and their 2 daughters at 244 Spring Bank adjacent to Botanic Railway station, which also housed his studio at the rear. The building was later owned by Fairburn Electrics.

Towards the end of the 19th century demand for William's style of sculpture dwindled and his business suffered. On Saturday 9th August 1902, at the age of 58, William shot himself in the head with a service rifle. William and his mother and father are all buried in the Hull General Cemetery, and although their headstone no longer remains, the East Yorkshire Family History Society recorded the inscriptions.

*Fig.19. Willian Day Keyworth.*

*Fig.20. Statue of William Wilberforce outside Wilberforce House executed by W.D.Keyworth.*

# Reverend William Clowes (1780-1851)

Fig.21.Tomb of William Clowes.

Born in Burslem, Staffordshire in 1780. His father was a local potter. His mother Ann was distantly related to Josiah Wedgwood and there is also a link to Charles Darwin. In his early life William was like many young men in that he liked to drink and gamble, probably to excess at times. This often led him into trouble. One trick it was said he used to do, was to pass himself off as a Press Gang member, the notorious method used by the government of the time to recruit people to serve in the Royal Navy. This prank probably wouldn't have endeared him to others in the inns and public houses of his day and may have been quite a dangerous thing to do! However, on one occasion he himself was arrested by a Press Gang and this may have cured him of such practical joking.

He was converted to Methodism in about 1805. In 1807 he became a preacher, but quickly fell afoul of the traditionalists in the church and was expelled. This was not unexceptional as Methodism splintered rapidly into numerous groupings after the death of its founder, John Wesley.

William collaborated with a colleague, Hugh Bourne, and together they founded Primitive Methodism, which appears to have appealed to many at the time, especially in Northern England and also in the USA. As Hullwebs.co.uk states,

> *They differed from the other branches of Methodism in several ways; they emphasised the work of lay people rather than ordained ministers; they encouraged female preachers; they rejected the Anglican influence on worship, preferring simplicity; and they stressed the political implications of the Christian message, where the Wesleyans were nervous of political involvement.*

Clowes arrived in Hull in 1819 and chose to stay in the town after his missionary work had ended in 1842. He died in March 1851. In 1898 a tomb was erected to his memory in what has become known as 'Prim Corner' due to the number of influential and devoted members of this particular church being buried there. In 2019 it is hoped to celebrate the bi-centenary of his arrival in Hull not only locally, but nationally too.

*Fig.22. Early photograph of Clowes' tomb after erection in 1898.*

# William Warden (1817-1879)

*Fig.23. Portrait of William Warden.*

William Warden is a forgotten hero of the town of Hull. His persistence, engineering skills and knowledge, led finally to Hull having a clean source of water that we still enjoy today.

The trials and tribulations that this issue created are well documented elsewhere. Suffice to say that William Warden and others were unhappy at how the corporation had spent a large amount of money on the improvement of the Stoneferry Waterworks, near where Reservoir Road now stands, only for it to still produce unclean water. This was understandable, as the water was drawn from the River Hull, which was also the major sewer for not just Hull but all the towns and villages that were sited upstream, including Beverley and Driffield. In effect, Hull was using sewage-tainted water and the technology of the time could not eradicate it, thus leading to the spread of disease and ultimately the death of its inhabitants.

William Warden wrote to the corporation stating that he could produce enough water for the town of Hull from well borings at Springhead. Indeed, he offered to the Corporation a deal that he would get 5,000,000 gallons of fresh water from these well borings. If he produced this amount, he asked for £500 and his expenses paid. If he failed, he would receive nothing. The corporation were unwilling to enter such a transaction as they had already spent heavily on the Stoneferry project.

Eventually public pressure and the active encouragement of some councillors forced the corporation to accept this generous offer from William. By 1860 he achieved his promise to the corporation and fresh water was available to the inhabitants of Hull.

Of course, this wasn't the end of the matter and eventually he had to go to court to get the corporation to pay him his money. Finally, in 1861 he was paid £1500 which ironically came to about £300 less than his expenses, so William actually lost money on this venture. The corporation had spent about £92,000 on the Stoneferry project. However, the end result was what counted and his fellows, for giving them all the gift of clean water, feted William Warden, in later years.

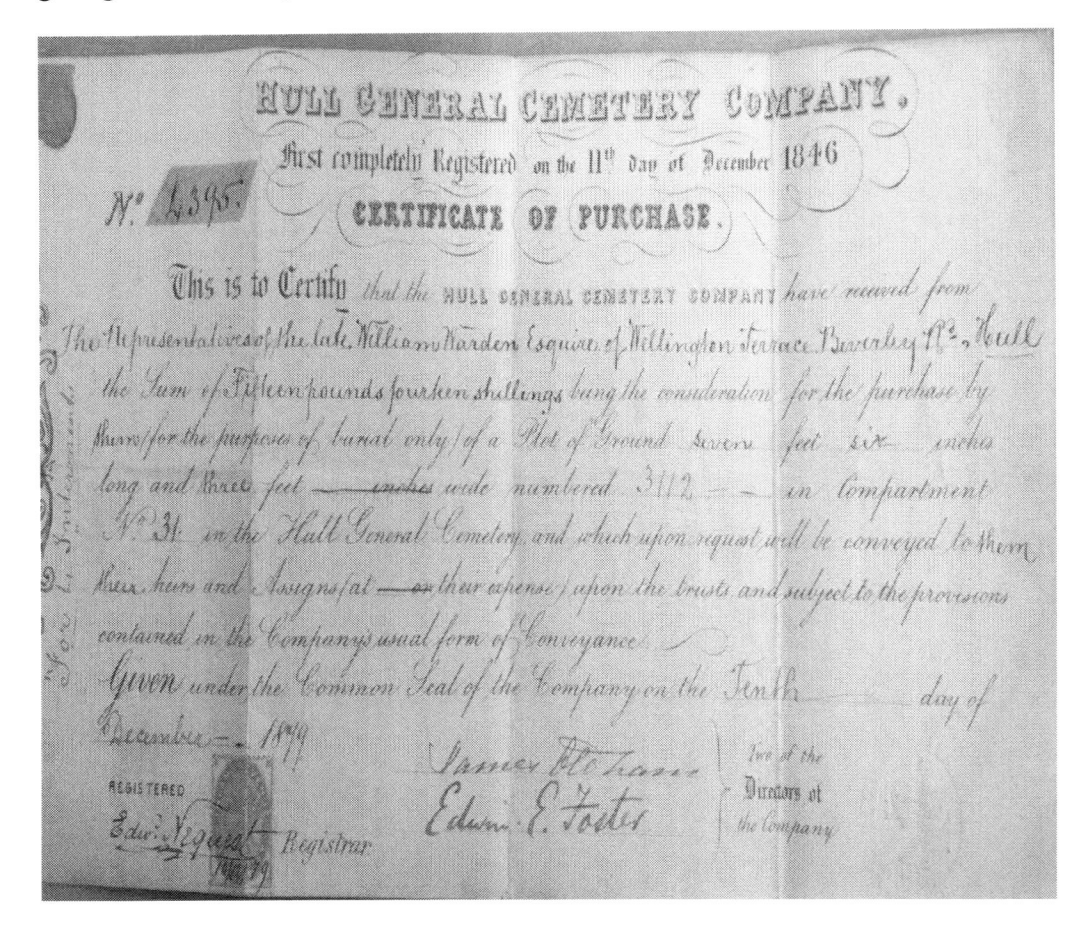

*Fig.24. Burial certificate of William Warden, dated 1879.*

## Mayors/Lord Mayors

There are upwards of 13 mayors and lord mayors buried in Hull General Cemetery. Two have already been mentioned, in Henry Hodge and Zachariah Pearson. Others are William Hodge, Henry's brother, and Kelburne King, who was a respected doctor and held the post of surgeon to the Infirmary, In the fevered world of Ripperology, that is the constant searching for the identity of Jack the Ripper, Kelburne King is said to have treated one of the suspects for a gunshot wound. Another mayor, Henry Blundell will be discussed later. Here are two more individuals who shaped the present city that is Kingston upon Hull:

## Thomas Thompson (1784-1865)

One of the most outspoken and benevolent characters of the first half of 19th century Hull was Thomas Thompson. Born in Long Haughton, near Alnwick to poor parents, Thomas was a farm labourer with no formal education, and in 1797, aged only 13, decided to seek his fortune in Hull where his maternal great uncle, Mr Thomas Nesbitt, had a cheese, bacon and salt merchants' shop in High Street After his uncle's death, the business was taken over by the manager, a Mr Marshall who encouraged Thomas to learn the business. Thomas eventually married Mr Marshall's daughter, Ann Elizabeth Jarvis, in Holy Trinity in 1809. They initially lived down Humber Dock Street and had ten children, only four of whom, survived him.

With the encouragement of his father in law, Thomas decided to branch out on his own, and after a somewhat shaky start, began importing fruit from Hamburg, later expanding the business into importing hides from Russia and India. By 1820 he had become a successful merchant, and ship owner, trading all around the globe. Despite his lack of formal education, Thomas became an alderman and JP. of the town, and was one of the earliest members of the newly reformed corporation. He was twice elected mayor, once in 1841 and again in 1857. He was also for many years, the Austrian vice consul due to his trading contacts.

*Fig.25. An early photograph of Thomas Thompson.*

Described as a hard-working man with the interests of Hull always at heart, he was very aware of his lack of education, and was often rebuked for his bluntness and egotistical manner. However, he cared passionately about the poor and the working-class people of Hull and gave money and coals to charity regularly.

He was instrumental in building the new workhouse on Anlaby Road, and the demolition of the old unsanitary one located in Whitefriargate. He was also very active in his support for the new waterworks at Stoneferry, laying the foundation stone in 1844, insisting that baths for the poor be incorporated using the surplus heat from the boilers for hot water. He later also supported William Warden in his endeavours to erect the waterworks at Springhead.

From the 1860's until the time of his death, he and his family lived at Cliff House, near the foreshore in Hessle. He was still active in the corporation until the time of his death, which occurred at the Swan Hotel in Harrogate whilst staying there to recuperate from a short illness.

His funeral cortege of a gothic hearse and three mourning coaches left Cliff House, Hessle and continued down Anlaby Road and into Elm Tree Ave (Park Street), along Spring Bank where it was met by a large number of private carriages belonging to corporation dignitaries (including the mayor) and a great number of merchants and tradesmen. The monument to Thomas and his family still survives in Hull General Cemetery.

# John Leak (1831-1895)

A man, who was the mayor of Hull four times, is buried in Hull General Cemetery. John Leak was born at Youlham Lodge, near York, in 1831. He was articled to a York firm of solicitors and moved to Hull, where he worked for Mr Edward Cleathing Bell who had a practice in Bowlalley Lane, eventually becoming a partner in the firm. He later formed a partnership with Alderman Roberts, (Roberts & Leak) and still later a new firm by the name of Leak, Till & Stephenson also situated in Bowlalley Lane.

He married Ann Wade Oglesby, the daughter of Richard Ogelsby, glass & china merchant of Humber Street in 1862 and had one daughter, Gertrude in 1864. The family lived at 92 Beverley Road, which was the right-hand side house of a terrace of four at the corner of Harley Street. Unfortunately, the house was destroyed in WW2. John became interested in local politics and became a councillor in 1875, and after the death of his partner, Alderman Roberts, was elected alderman in 1878. Two years later in 1880 he became mayor for the first time, a position he would hold for 3 consecutive years 1880, 81 and 82, and was elected mayor again in 1886.

As a Board Director of the Hull & Barnsley Railway, he was instrumental in the construction of Alexandra Dock, which was opened in 1885. He was chief magistrate of the town and supported many charitable undertakings; he was also actively involved with the Victoria Children's Hospital in Park Street. As Mayor, he opened the East Park in the Jubilee Year of 1887, and the 'old' Market Hall in Market Place and was a keen sportsman and founder member of the Hull Cricket Club.

*Fig,26. Monument to John Leak.*

During his later years he suffered long-term ill health and died of heart problems in 1895, aged 64. His wife Ann died two years later of diabetes aged 62. His daughter Gertrude never married, and she also died of diabetes in 1905 aged 41. They are all buried in a family grave in Hull General Cemetery marked with a tall pink marble obelisk that still remains. The EYFHS Monumental Inscription Book incorrectly notes the name inscription, as 'Leake' not Leak.

# Sir James Reckitt (1833-1924)

The firm of Reckitts is known throughout the world, but its beginnings were in Hull and it continued to be the headquarters of the firm until very recently. The firm has been well documented elsewhere, as have the more famous members of the family that began this venture. However, Hull General Cemetery plays a small role in their lives.

The Reckitt family were Quakers and, as part of their religious beliefs, they felt that they could not be buried within consecrated ground. Prior to the Toleration Act of 1694 Quakers were treated as not only heretics but also as treasonous. This was due mainly to the fact that Quakers could not, due to religious beliefs, swear allegiance on the Bible to the Crown.

Life was difficult for the Quakers and death not much better as, mentioned above, burial within parish churchyards was not an option for them. In 1678 a merchant called Anthony Wells purchased some ground well outside of the town in the parish of Southcoates, where Hodgson Street now stands. There he opened a burial ground for his fellow Quakers. The authorities quickly suppressed it but it was eventually re-opened in the more tolerant period of William III and Mary.

From this period, it continued to provide burial places for the Quakers in the area until closed by Parliament, along with many other over-crowded parish burial grounds in the town in 1855. This led to the Quakers negotiating with the Hull General Cemetery to lease a part of the cemetery for their own burials and in 1855, a 999year lease was signed. It is in this section of the cemetery that influential and important Quakers such as Isaac and Sir James Reckitt are buried alongside members of the Priestman family including, William Dent Priestman, the inventor of the oil engine.

A lesser stone, tucked away on the path, celebrates someone perhaps even more important to the history of Hull, and that is the small stone dedicated to the memory of Eliza Wells, the wife of Anthony Wells. She died in childbirth in 1676 and it is due to her death, and the child sadly, that Anthony Wells purchased the original Quaker burial ground. That the stone survives is wonderful for, as we know, the Quakers were loath to advertise their presence due to society's fear of them and the reprisals this could incur on them. This stone therefore, with its historical provenance, is probably not just locally important but also nationally too.

*Fig.27. Quaker Burial Ground in Hull General Cemetery, 2016.*

*Fig.28. Early Quaker headstone.*

# John Fountain (1802-1887) and the 'Workhouse Mound'.

John Fountain, whose large obelisk marks the place of his burial, was born in 1802. In the 1840's in Hull he was a trader in fruit and fish. Indeed, many of the adverts of the period state that he is a 'Nut, Orange and Herring seller'. A somewhat unlikely combination even today in our 'foodie' society but quite common in those days. That he managed this trade very well is indicated in that by 1848 he had been elected to the corporation.

Always interested in the workings of the new Poor Law, he occupied the post of Guardian to the Hull Workhouse until his death and, as his stone testifies, the welfare of the paupers in his care were so dear to his heart he wanted to be buried in their midst. Indeed, John Fountain is perhaps indicative of the dichotomy that Victorian society felt about the poor and their dealings with them.

An early example from John's own life is that during the Irish Famine in 1847 he donated three guineas to the relief fund for this cause. Some three years later, however, he donated £20 to lobby parliament to offset an increase in port charges that Hull was facing. That he felt inclined to spend significantly more on this venture than in attempting to help forestall the deaths from the Irish Famine is difficult to justify in this day and age.

Another tale around the same time involved him taking a young man, aged 15 years, to the local court over the theft of a bag valued at one shilling and 10lbs of rope also valued at a shilling. The prisoner was undefended in the court and was sentenced to nine months imprisonment with hard labour and also to 'be twice privately whipped.'

Yes, it's easy to find such examples, not only for John Fountain, but also for many of the notables that graced Victorian Britain. It is this apparent difficulty by the

Victorians to understand that poverty was not a crime, that so sets us

*Fig.29. Monument to John Fountain, 2016.*

*Fig.30. Covenant signed between the Hull Workhouse and Hull General Cemetery, 1859.*

apart from our recent ancestors. John wanted to be buried amongst his charges and this is commendable but maybe perhaps they might have preferred being treated kindlier in life.

John lived at a house in Balmoral Terrace, since demolished and ironically now part of the extensive buildings that form the Hull Royal Infirmary, which was once the site of the Hull Workhouse that John presided over for so long.

Fountain Street on Anlaby Road was named after him. John often provided fresh fruit from his trade networks to the inhabitants of the workhouse and he was also instrumental in changing the attire that workhouse inmates had to wear from a 'coarse material' to a more reasonable 'neat uniform' as the local newspapers reported.

The mound he sits upon is the burial place of perhaps upwards of 2 or 3,000 paupers from the Hull Workhouse. A covenant was signed between the cemetery company and the Hull Workhouse in 1859 allocating this particular section of the cemetery for the use of pauper burials.

Prior to this, the guardians purchased graves as and when they needed them, but this may have been problematic for the cemetery company as such graves would, of necessity due to the acknowledgement that they may be needed as and when, not be completely filled in after a burial. This could have caused a health and safety issue for the cemetery and placing the pauper graves at the far end of the cemetery may have suited both parties as the covenant appears to have allowed the workhouse a discount on the price of the graves.

# John Westall Widdas (1802-1858)

*Fig.31. Headstone of John Widdas, 2017.*

A little-known artist and hailing originally from Nottingham. His family had worked in the lace industry there for at least two generations. Obviously, his family were itinerant, as he was baptized at Darlington and he married in Leeds in 1823.

By 1828 he was making a living as an artist and there is a belief that he was self-taught. John unfortunately must have fallen on hard times and eventually died in Hull Workhouse, seemingly of old age or 'decay of nature' as the Victorians used to like to term it.

One of his children was Richard Dodd Widdas who painted the scene of the Diana trapped in the ice, on show in Hull Maritime Museum. Ironically, Richard, by far the more famous of the two, had his headstone removed in the 1970's clearance whilst his father's headstone still remains.

*Fig.32. Self portrait of John Widdas.*

# Henry Blundell (1789-1865)

Henry Blundell, born at Lincoln, spent all of his working life in Hull raising himself from a humble apprenticeship to a brush maker, up to the dizzy heights of being the chairman of a large exporting business.

The name Blundell, Spence and Co. is linked closely with Hull and it was this man who founded the first link. In 1811 Henry entered into partnership with his brother-in-law, William Spence to produce colour and paint. Probably striking at the right time, their products were eagerly sought after by the aspiring middle class, who could not afford the Chinese wallpaper the gentry used.

The business flourished and new sites were set up but the main site was the one first used at the junction between Spring Bank, Beverley Road and Prospect Street, still called today, 'Blundell's Corner'.

In the 1830's Henry patented new machinery for processing oil from linseed which added another income stream to the firm. Candle manufacture was also a good source of income for the firm as lighting at that period still depended upon such means.

Henry Blundell retired from an active role in the business in 1864 but his hope for a long and happy retirement was doomed to failure, as he died some four months later in January 1865. His house on Beverley Road, known as Brunswick House, stood at the top of Brunswick Avenue and one remaining gatepost still stands to remind us of what once stood there.

Henry named his house after a popular type of paint his firm produced in the 1830's called Brunswick Green, but it was commonly called 'Blundell's Green' due to its popularity.

*Fig.33. Henry Blundell as a young man.*

# The Blind Institute

Three notable Hull men who were jointly responsible for improving the welfare of the blind in Hull, are buried in Hull General Cemetery. In 1863 a Dr Moon, a blind man from Kent, was visiting a friend in Hull. He called into Joseph Coultas

Akester's chemist shop at 77 Hessle Road, not far from the Alexandra pub. In conversation, Dr Moon explained to Joseph that he had developed a new reading system that enabled the blind to read (although this was 15 years after Louis Braille had developed his system), he called the system Moon Code. Joseph was so impressed by the system that he discussed it with his friend Alderman Charles Richard Lambert, brother of the Lambert wine merchants, and after whom Lambert Street is named, and who was also blind.

*Fig.34. The original Blind Institution.*

Alderman Lambert was also so taken with the alphabet that the following year, in conjunction with his with friend and neighbour, ophthalmic surgeon Dr William Craven Rockliffe, he created a 'home' for blind women at 83 Charles Street, with a workshop around the corner in Kingston Square, in the old Institute building. (Dr Rockliffe had changed his name from Lunn a few years earlier for inheritance reasons) The employees made produce, mainly baskets, which they sold to earn a living.

*Fig.35. Headstone of William Craven Rockliffe.*

In 1920 they moved to larger premises on Beverley Road, called Beech Holme, the former home of Hull ship-owner Edward Leetham (1837-1918), who had died 2 years earlier with no children. The name of the house was changed to The Rockliffe Home for Blind Women and remains to this day.

Alderman Lambert died in 1881 aged 64 and is buried with his wife Emma and family in Hull General Cemetery, as is Joseph Coultas Akester and his family. So too is William Craven Rockliffe who died in 1930 aged 81 and is buried with his wife Agnes in Hull General Cemetery.

# Henry Redmore (1820-1887)

Henry Redmore is recognised as one of Britain's finest maritime painters. He was born in Hull in 1820, the son of James and Mary Redmore (nee Wilkinson). He trained as a Marine Engineer, and spent some years at sea, where he made observations of ships and learned to sketch them.

He married Martha Markham in 1844 and had four children. The family lived close to his parents in Cottingham Terrace, between Charles Street and Norfolk Street. By 1848 he was advertising himself as an artist in trade directories.

There is some speculation he received instruction from John Ward, another noted Hull painter. He later exhibited at the Royal Academy. His wife, Martha died in 1869 and the following year, he married widow Ann Hopwood, who lived at 163 Coltman Street, close to Henry's studio in Regent Street. Henry moved into the

Coltman Street house and lived there until his death.

*Fig.36. Henry Redmore.*

*Fig.37. Headstone of Henry Redmore, 2016.*

Many of his subjects are of ships moored in the Humber and surrounding areas, including Scarborough and Whitby, the quality of which compare with his contemporary, John Ward, who died in the cholera epidemic in 1849. Hull Maritime Museum has several examples of his work.

One of his sons, Edward King Redmore, was also a maritime painter, but not of the same standard as his father. Henry died in 1887 aged 67, and is buried in Hull General Cemetery, the service being performed by the Rev Sibree. The headstone still remains, and his house at 163 Coltman Street has been awarded a blue plaque.

Recent sales of his works have reached figures of between £350,000 and half a million pounds.

These are just a few of the noted people who are buried in the Cemetery but space is limited and perhaps you'd want to go exploring for yourselves so here are a few other notables you might like to find.

**Reverend William Kemp,** who built and owned Thanet House. This house later became Park Street College

**George Parker**, copper merchant who donated the lectern that is still used in the Hull Minster today and who later went bankrupt.

**Thomas Holmes**, of Holmes Tannery fame.

**Doctor Gordon**, the 'people's friend', noted Temperance advocate and whose headstone was also erected as a result of public subscription.

**Reverend Thomas Stratten and his son Thomas**. The elder Thomas was a forceful minister of the church whilst his son was one of the major founders of Newland Homes and also a leading figure in the creation of the board schools of Hull after the legislation of 1870 allowed them to be built.

**Timothy Reeves**, the grandfather of Sir John Ellerman, of Ellerman Wilson line fame who at one point was deemed to be the richest man in the world.

**Samuel Lighfoot**, an early investor in the railways and one of the original subscribers to the Wilberforce Monument. He lived at Springhead Hall, which is now Springhead Golf Course clubhouse.

**Joseph Wright**, architect, **William Hodge**, Henry's brother who was famous in his own right, **Benjamin Hudson**, noted artist and many, many more of the 'movers and shakers' of Victorian Hull.

Of course, the nature of the cemetery was seen as basically democratic so there are stories regarding more unfortunate souls the cemetery contained. Below is a photograph of the headstone recording the deaths of some of the poor orphaned children who were in the care of the Port of Hull Society for Sailors' Orphans that eventually became sited at the complex known as Newland Homes.

These children were never to live the full life some other people discussed in this booklet did, but their names are recorded and their short lives memorialised which would never have happened in the churchyards the Hull General Cemetery replaced. Another, perhaps forgotten, aspect which should make us all proud of the role this cemetery played during its life. It could, and sometimes did, give a measure of equality, if not in life, then at least in death.

*Fig.38. Port of Hull Society's headstone.*

# **Conclusion**

Hull General Cemetery is one of the greatest historical resources that the city of Hull has. That it has been abused, neglected and damaged by its custodians is not in doubt but it still breathes charm and exudes magic. Walking there, within 100 yards of a major thoroughfare, one can forget the modern world.

You can experience the pleasure of a 'country walk' whilst being ten minutes away from the lattes and pastries of Princes Avenue. You can emulate Dr Who and time travel simply by reading the inscriptions and wonder at the lives and times of those people who were buried here. You can bird watch in solitude, feed the many squirrels or simply try to identify the many plants and trees there and all within a short walk from 'civilization'.

But beware, the future of this unique paradise within our city is fragile, due to our neglect, both individual and corporate, and once this fabulous historical resource has gone, it cannot be recreated. It has suffered in its recent history but it is still here, thankfully.

Now it should be treasured by us. If you have an interest in this city's past it is invaluable. In its way it offers as much as Wilberforce House and Hull Minster do to the story of Hull. All are important to any study of Hull's history; all have played their part in the city's past and hopefully they all will in the future too.

*Fig.39. Hull General Cemetery Gates, Spring Bank West, 2016.*

The Hull General Cemetery offers a rare insight into the world of Victorian Hull and we are so close to losing the unique opportunity that it presents to us.

We owe it, not only to the people buried there who deserve our respect, but also to the citizens of tomorrow's Hull to preserve their city's history today.

## Select Bibliography for Further Reference:

**Sections:**

*General:*

**A History of Hull,** Gillett E., & K.A.MacMahon, The University of Hull Press, 1989.

**A History of the County of York East Riding, Volume 1,** K.J.Allison (Ed.), Oxford University Press, 1969.

*Hull General Cemetery:*

'A Walk Round the Spring Bank Cemetery' in **Kingstonia,** J.Symons, The Eastern Morning News Company, 1889.

'The Genesis of the Hull General Cemetery' by Pete Lowden in **Hull Civic Newsletter**, June 2016, June & October, 2017, February & May 2018,

Chapter 6, in **Fifty Years' Recollections of Hull**, James Sibree, A.Brown & Sons Ltd., 1884.

*Notables:*

**Zachariah Pearson: Man of Hull,** Marian Shaw, The Grimsay Press, 2016.

**River and Spring,** Mary Fowler, Highgate Publications, 1997.

**Marine Painting in Hull Through Three Centuries,** Arthur G Credland, Hutton Press, 1993.

**Artists and Craftsmen of Hull and East Yorkshire,** Arthur G. Credland, Hull Museums, 2000

**The History of Reckitt and Sons Ltd,** Basil N. Reckitt, A. Brown and Sons, 1952.

**Keep The Home Fires Burning,** John Markham (Ed), Highgate Publications, 1988.

**Hull Maritime Paintings,** The Ferens Art Gallery, Hull Museums, 1985.

**The Diana of Hull,** Arthur G. Credland, Hull Museums, 1979.

**William Dent Priestman of Hull and the First Oil Engine,** James Dent Priestman, The University of Hull, 1994.

**The Blundell Book, 1811-1951: A Short History,** Blundell, Spence and Co., Ltd., Beck and Inchbold, 1951.

**Fred Ewell: A Life in Art,** Wendy Loncaster & Malcolm Shields, 2014.

## Acknowledgements:

Hull Museums, Guildhall, Hull: *Fig.6*

Lee's Rest Homes, Anlaby Road, & Fred Ewell: A Life in Art: *Fig.8*

Artists and Craftsmen of Hull and East Yorkshire: *Fig. 17.*

Lee's Rest Homes website: *Fig 9*

Bill Longbone: *Figs.18,19,20,25,34,37*

Pete Lowden: *Front cover and back cover.*

*Figs.2,3,5,7,10,11,12,14,15,16,21,22,26,27,28,29,31,35,38,39.*

Hull History Centre: *Figs.,1,24,30.*

Marine Painting in Hull Through Three Centuries: *Fig. 36.*

Hull Daily Mail: *Fig.4.*

The Diana of Hull; *Fig.13*

Hull Maritime Museum: *Fig.32.*

The Blundell Book, 1811-1951: *Fig.33.*

All rights reserved.

No part of this publication may be reproduced or transmitted in any form, or by any means, electronic, mechanical or otherwise, without the express permission of the authors.

**The authors**:

The two authors have long and significant links with the cemetery.

Bill is a relative by marriage to one of the notables mentioned in the text; Michael Kelly. He has also contributed many rare images and a great deal of quality research to various local history websites, some of them relating to the cemetery.

Pete also has relatives buried there, but none quite as grand as Bill's. However, Pete can claim to have worked in the cemetery when he was a young man, watched the destruction of it from the inside, and that may have stirred his desire to investigate and record its history.

They decided to pool their research for this venture to aid The Friends of Hull General Cemetery in their aim to raise the profile of Hull General Cemetery not only locally but hopefully on a wider stage. All proceeds from this book will go to the above organization to fund ongoing projects of improvements.

Printed in Poland
by Amazon Fulfillment
Poland Sp. z o.o., Wrocław